Learning to Read, Step by Step!

Ready to Read Preschool–Kindergarten
• big type and easy words • rhyme and rhythm • picture clues
For children who know the alphabet and are eager to begin reading.

Reading with Help Preschool–Grade 1
• basic vocabulary • short sentences • simple stories
For children who recognize familiar words and sound out new words with help.

Reading on Your Own Grades 1–3
• engaging characters • easy-to-follow plots • popular topics
For children who are ready to read on their own.

Reading Paragraphs Grades 2–3
• challenging vocabulary • short paragraphs • exciting stories
For newly independent readers who read simple sentences with confidence.

Ready for Chapters Grades 2–4
• chapters • longer paragraphs • full-color art
For children who want to take the plunge into chapter books but still like colorful pictures.

STEP INTO READING® is designed to give every child a successful reading experience. The grade levels are only guides; children will progress through the steps at their own speed, developing confidence in their reading. The F&P Text Level on the back cover serves as another tool to help you choose the right book for your child.

Remember, a lifetime love of reading starts with a single step!

For Carla and Haley, who are carved into my heart—
forever. And thank you to my editor, Anna Membrino,
for her patience, partnership, and creativity—
I love collaborating with you!
Thanks to Maribeth Batcho's 2013–2014 second-
grade class and to Mike Muncer for help in reading
drafts along the way!
—F.M.

For Roy Sharp, an ace among uncles
—R.W.

Text copyright © 2015 by Frank Murphy
Cover art and interior illustrations copyright © 2015 by Richard Walz

All rights reserved. Published in the United States by Random House Children's Books, a division of Penguin Random House LLC, New York.

Step into Reading, Random House, and the Random House colophon are registered trademarks of Penguin Random House LLC.

Photograph credit: p. 48: found on Wikimedia Commons.

Visit us on the Web!
StepIntoReading.com
randomhousekids.com

Educators and librarians, for a variety of teaching tools, visit us at RHTeachersLibrarians.com

Library of Congress Cataloging-in-Publication Data
Murphy, Frank.
Take a hike, Teddy Roosevelt! / by Frank Murphy ; illustrated by Richard Walz.
pages cm. — (Step into reading, step 3)
ISBN 978-0-375-86937-2 (trade pbk.) — ISBN 978-0-375-96937-9 (lib. bdg.) — ISBN 978-0-375-98322-1 (ebook)
1. Roosevelt, Theodore, 1858–1919. 2. Presidents—United States—Biography.
3. Conservationists—United States—Biography. I. Walz, Richard, illustrator. II. Title.
E757.M946 2015 973.911092—dc23 [B] 2014048136

Printed in the United States of America
10 9 8 7 6 5 4 3 2 1

This book has been officially leveled by using the F&P Text Level Gradient™ Leveling System.

Take a Hike, Teddy Roosevelt!

by Frank Murphy
illustrated by Richard Walz

Random House 🏠 New York

Jefferson

Washington

America has had over
forty presidents.
These four did
such BIG things
that their faces are carved
into Mount Rushmore.

Roosevelt

Lincoln

You might not recognize
the third guy.
His name was
Theodore Roosevelt,
but people called him Teddy.

If it weren't for Teddy,
people would have
destroyed many of America's
forests and other national treasures.

This story is about how Teddy
protected America's environment.

Teddy was born in 1858
in New York City.
There was
lots of pollution.
Teddy had asthma,
which made it hard
for him to breathe.

To help his lungs grow stronger,

his parents took him

to the country,

where the air was fresh.

His parents told him,

"Take a hike, Teddy!"

So he did!

Teddy rode horses.

He swam and rowed.

He climbed trees
and hiked hills.

10

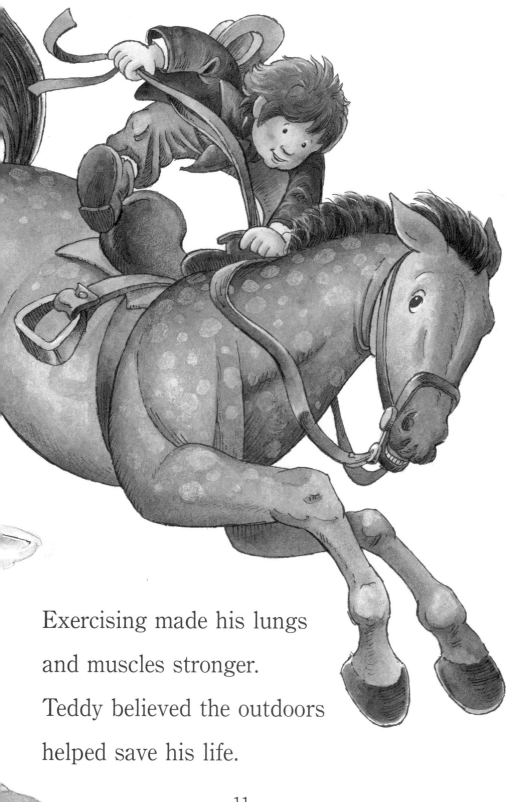

Exercising made his lungs
and muscles stronger.
Teddy believed the outdoors
helped save his life.

Teddy loved being outdoors
and was interested in wildlife.
When he was hiking,
he took a notebook.

He observed animals
and insects.
He wrote down everything
he noticed about them.

Teddy didn't stop there.
He started collecting insects
and animals.
He kept spiders and ants
and ladybugs in his bedroom.

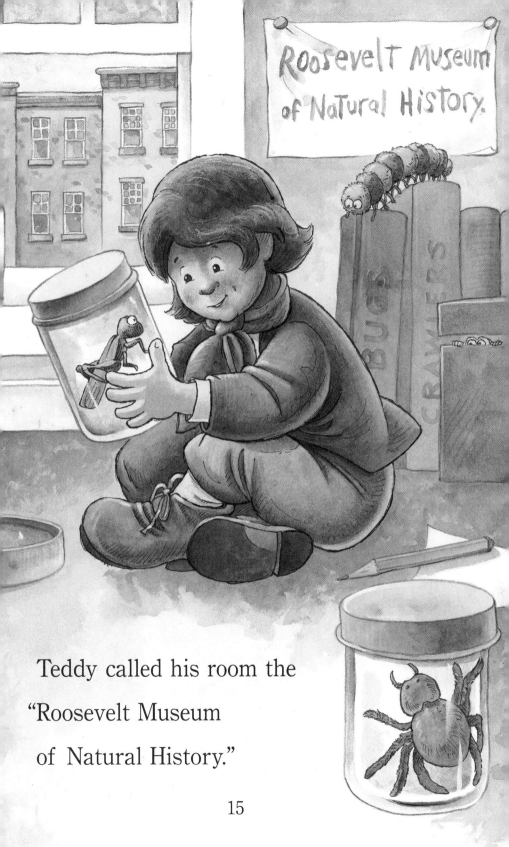

Teddy called his room the
"Roosevelt Museum
of Natural History."

15

Soon Teddy's little museum
became too big
for his bedroom.
He hid a litter of field mice
in an icebox.

He tied a snapping turtle to
a sink in the laundry room.
His frogs and snakes escaped
from boxes and buckets.

Once Teddy and his friend Fred
were out collecting animals.
Teddy found a frog.
But he had run out of room
in his boxes!
So Teddy put the frog
inside his hat.

Soon a carriage came by
and stopped.

It was Governor Fish
and his wife, Mrs. Fish!

Fred tipped his hat to say hello.

Teddy didn't want to be rude,

so he tipped his hat too!

When Teddy went off to college,
nature was still on his mind.
He studied natural history
and zoology.

He kept animals and insects
in his college room.
He even shared his room
with a giant turtle.
His landlord was not happy!

Teddy wanted to do
BIG things one day.
But he wasn't sure
that studying animals and nature
would help him do those BIG things.

So Teddy decided to
study government.

After college
Teddy worked in the
New York State government.
But he missed the outdoors,
and he still suffered
from asthma.

He remembered what
his parents had said:
"Take a hike, Teddy!"
So he did!

Teddy left for the
American West.
He rode horses
and raised cattle.
He studied the stars
while he wrote a book.

After two years
of living on the frontier,
he had gained
thirty pounds of muscle
and his asthma was gone forever!

But something else
happened to Teddy.
In the West,
he saw that people
were using too many of
America's natural resources.

They were chopping down
more trees than they needed.
They were building railroads,
stores, and towns.
Some of the most beautiful
places in the country were
being destroyed.

There was something else
that bothered Teddy.
Back then,
people hunted wild animals
for food and for sport.
But Teddy saw that people were
hunting more than they needed.
Some animals were in danger
of becoming extinct.

Millions of bison
once roamed wild.
When Teddy arrived
in the West,
there were only
about three hundred left!
He knew he had to do
BIG things to help
America's environment.

Teddy decided to start small.
He went back home
and worked to become the
governor of New York.

He protected the forests.
He passed laws to help
stop pollution in the city.

In 1901,

Teddy became

America's twenty-sixth president.

No president had ever
made protecting America's
environment important.
But Teddy did!

Teddy and his family moved
into the White House.
As always,
his new home
became a mini-zoo.
Teddy and his children
had lots of pets.

Rabbits, birds, guinea pigs,
ponies, cats, dogs,
a badger, and even a bear
named Jonathan Edwards!

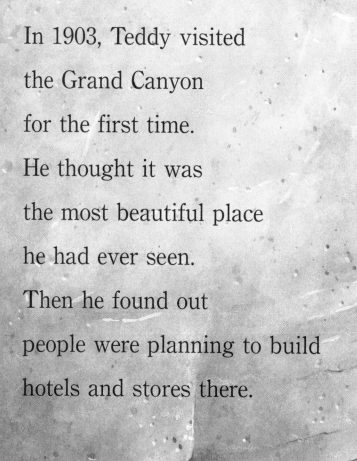

In 1903, Teddy visited
the Grand Canyon
for the first time.
He thought it was
the most beautiful place
he had ever seen.
Then he found out
people were planning to build
hotels and stores there.

Teddy wanted people
to see the Grand Canyon's
natural beauty forever.
The way he saw it
for the first time.

After his visit to the Grand Canyon,
Teddy knew he had to do something.
He had to protect
America's great outdoors.
He started signing bills
to protect America's
wildlife and large parts
of its environment.

But sometimes

people tried to stop these bills.

This didn't stop Teddy!

He signed a law that gave him

the power to make any land

a national monument.

Then Teddy found out that
birds were in danger in Florida.
People were killing them
and using their feathers
in fancy hats.

Teddy asked if there was a law
that stopped the president
from protecting this land.
There wasn't!
"Very well then," Teddy said.
"I so declare it!"

Teddy had just made America's
first wildlife refuge.
Now no one could stop him
from saving America's
natural resources and wildlife.

Teddy created
5 national parks,
18 national monuments,
150 national forests,
and 51 bird sanctuaries.
When he was done,
he had protected over
230 million acres of land—
forever.

Now go visit
one of these great places
and take a hike—
just like Teddy!

October 27, 1858–January 6, 1919

Author's Note

Teddy was the first president to really care about conservation. He said, "We must handle the water, the wood, the grasses, so that we will hand them on to our children and children's children in better and not worse shape than we got them."

And he even helped pass laws to protect the bison. Now there are almost 300,000 bison roaming free in America!